Date: _____

Today I am grateful for

_____

_____

_____

To Do List

- ☐
- ☐
- ☐
- ☐

Chores

_____

_____

_____

My water intake

Notes

_____

_____

_____

_____

Remember	Breakfast	Lunch	Dinner

Date: _____

Today I am grateful for

_____

_____

To Do List

☐

☐

☐

☐

Chores

_____

_____

_____

_____

My water intake

Notes

_____

_____

_____

_____

Remember	Breakfast	Lunch	Dinner

Date: _____

Today I am grateful for

_____
_____

To Do List

- ☐
- ☐
- ☐
- ☐

Chores

_____
_____
_____
_____

My water intake

Notes

_____
_____
_____
_____
_____
_____

Remember	Breakfast	Lunch	Dinner

Date: _____

Today I am grateful for

_____

_____

To Do List

☐

☐

☐

☐

Chores

_____

_____

_____

My water intake

Notes

_____

_____

_____

_____

_____

| Remember | Breakfast | Lunch | Dinner |

Date: _____

Today I am grateful for

_____

_____

_____

To Do List

☐

☐

☐

☐

Chores

_____

_____

_____

_____

My water intake

Notes

_____

_____

_____

_____

_____

Remember	Breakfast	Lunch	Dinner

Date: _____

Today I am grateful for

_____

_____

_____

To Do List

- [ ]
- [ ]
- [ ]
- [ ]

Chores

_____

_____

_____

My water intake

Notes

_____

_____

_____

_____

_____

_____

Remember	Breakfast	Lunch	Dinner

Date: _____

Today I am grateful for

_____

_____

_____

To Do List

- [ ]
- [ ]
- [ ]
- [ ]

Chores

_____

_____

_____

_____

My water intake

Notes

_____

_____

_____

_____

_____

Remember	Breakfast	Lunch	Dinner

Date: _____

Today I am grateful for

_____

_____

To Do List

☐
☐
☐
☐

Chores

_____
_____
_____
_____

My water intake

Notes

_____
_____
_____
_____
_____

| Remember | Breakfast | Lunch | Dinner |

Date: _____

Today I am grateful for

_____

_____

To Do List

☐

☐

☐

☐

Chores

_____

_____

_____

_____

My water intake

Notes

_____

_____

_____

_____

Remember	Breakfast	Lunch	Dinner

Date: _____

Today I am grateful for

_____

_____

_____

To Do List

- ☐
- ☐
- ☐
- ☐

Chores

_____
_____
_____
_____

My water intake

Notes

_____
_____
_____
_____
_____
_____

| Remember | Breakfast | Lunch | Dinner |

Date: _____

Today I am grateful for

_____

_____

To Do List

- ☐
- ☐
- ☐
- ☐

Chores

_____

_____

_____

_____

My water intake

Notes

_____

_____

_____

_____

_____

Remember	Breakfast	Lunch	Dinner

Date: _____

Today I am grateful for

_____

_____

_____

To Do List

- [ ]
- [ ]
- [ ]
- [ ]

Chores

_____

_____

_____

_____

My water intake

Notes

_____

_____

_____

_____

_____

| Remember | Breakfast | Lunch | Dinner |

Date: _____

Today I am grateful for

_____

_____

_____

To Do List

☐
☐
☐
☐

Chores

_____
_____
_____
_____

My water intake

Notes

_____
_____
_____
_____
_____
_____

Remember	Breakfast	Lunch	Dinner

Date: _____

Today I am grateful for

_____

_____

To Do List

☐
☐
☐
☐

Chores

_____
_____
_____
_____

My water intake

Notes

_____
_____
_____
_____
_____

| Remember | Breakfast | Lunch | Dinner |

Date: _____

Today I am grateful for

_____

_____

_____

To Do List

☐
☐
☐
☐

Chores

_____
_____
_____
_____

My water intake

Notes

_____
_____
_____
_____

Remember	Breakfast	Lunch	Dinner

Date: _____

Today I am grateful for

_____

_____

To Do List

- ☐
- ☐
- ☐
- ☐

Chores

_____

_____

_____

My water intake

Notes

_____

_____

_____

_____

_____

Remember	Breakfast	Lunch	Dinner

Date: _____

Today I am grateful for

_____

_____

To Do List

☐

☐

☐

☐

Chores

_____

_____

_____

_____

My water intake

Notes

_____

_____

_____

_____

_____

Remember	Breakfast	Lunch	Dinner

Date: _____

Today I am grateful for

_____

_____

_____

To Do List

☐

☐

☐

☐

Chores

_____

_____

_____

My water intake

Notes

_____

_____

_____

_____

_____

Remember	Breakfast	Lunch	Dinner

Date: _____

Today I am grateful for

_____
_____

To Do List

☐
☐
☐
☐

Chores

_____
_____
_____
_____

My water intake

Notes

_____
_____
_____
_____
_____

Remember	Breakfast	Lunch	Dinner

Date: _____

Today I am grateful for

_____

_____

_____

To Do List

☐

☐

☐

☐

Chores

_____

_____

_____

_____

My water intake

Notes

_____

_____

_____

_____

_____

Remember	Breakfast	Lunch	Dinner

Date: _____

Today I am grateful for

_____

_____

To Do List

☐

☐

☐

☐

Chores

_____

_____

_____

_____

My water intake

Notes

_____

_____

_____

_____

_____

| Remember | Breakfast | Lunch | Dinner |

Date: _____

Today I am grateful for

_____

_____

_____

To Do List

☐

☐

☐

☐

Chores

_____

_____

_____

My water intake

Notes

_____

_____

_____

_____

_____

| Remember | Breakfast | Lunch | Dinner |

Date: _____

Today I am grateful for

_____

_____

_____

To Do List

☐

☐

☐

☐

Chores

_____

_____

_____

_____

My water intake

Notes

_____

_____

_____

_____

_____

Remember	Breakfast	Lunch	Dinner

Date: _____

Today I am grateful for

_____
_____

To Do List

☐
☐
☐
☐

Chores

_____
_____
_____
_____

My water intake

Notes

_____
_____
_____
_____
_____

Remember	Breakfast	Lunch	Dinner

Date: _____

Today I am grateful for

_____

_____

_____

To Do List

- ☐
- ☐
- ☐
- ☐

Chores

_____

_____

_____

_____

My water intake

Notes

_____

_____

_____

_____

_____

_____

Remember	Breakfast	Lunch	Dinner

Date: _____

Today I am grateful for

_____
_____
_____

To Do List

☐
☐
☐
☐

Chores

_____
_____
_____
_____

My water intake

Notes

_____
_____
_____
_____
_____

| Remember | Breakfast | Lunch | Dinner |

Date: _____

Today I am grateful for

_____
_____
_____

To Do List

☐
☐
☐
☐

Chores

_____
_____
_____
_____

My water intake

Notes

_____
_____
_____
_____
_____

Remember	Breakfast	Lunch	Dinner

Date: _____

Today I am grateful for

_____

_____

_____

To Do List

- ☐
- ☐
- ☐
- ☐

Chores

_____

_____

_____

My water intake

Notes

_____

_____

_____

_____

_____

| Remember | Breakfast | Lunch | Dinner |

Date: _____

Today I am grateful for

_____

_____

_____

To Do List

☐
☐
☐
☐

Chores

_____
_____
_____
_____

My water intake

Notes

_____
_____
_____
_____
_____

| Remember | Breakfast | Lunch | Dinner |

Date: _____

Today I am grateful for

_____

_____

To Do List

- ☐
- ☐
- ☐
- ☐

Chores

_____

_____

_____

My water intake

Notes

_____

_____

_____

_____

_____

| Remember | Breakfast | Lunch | Dinner |

Date: _____

Today I am grateful for

_____
_____

To Do List

☐
☐
☐
☐

Chores

_____
_____
_____
_____

My water intake

Notes

_____
_____
_____
_____
_____

| Remember | Breakfast | Lunch | Dinner |

Date: _____

Today I am grateful for

_____
_____
_____

To Do List

☐
☐
☐
☐

Chores

_____
_____
_____

My water intake

Notes

_____
_____
_____
_____
_____

Remember	Breakfast	Lunch	Dinner

Date: _____

Today I am grateful for

_____

_____

_____

To Do List

- [ ]
- [ ]
- [ ]
- [ ]

Chores

_____

_____

_____

_____

My water intake

Notes

_____

_____

_____

_____

_____

Remember	Breakfast	Lunch	Dinner

Date: _____

Today I am grateful for

_____

_____

To Do List

☐
☐
☐
☐

Chores

_____
_____
_____

My water intake

Notes

_____
_____
_____
_____
_____

| Remember | Breakfast | Lunch | Dinner |

Date: _____

Today I am grateful for

_____

_____

To Do List

☐

☐

☐

☐

Chores

_____

_____

_____

My water intake

Notes

_____

_____

_____

_____

_____

Remember	Breakfast	Lunch	Dinner

Date: _____

Today I am grateful for

_____

_____

To Do List

☐
☐
☐
☐

Chores

_____
_____
_____
_____

My water intake

Notes

_____
_____
_____
_____
_____
_____

| Remember | Breakfast | Lunch | Dinner |

Date: _____

Today I am grateful for

_____

_____

_____

To Do List

☐
☐
☐
☐

Chores

_____

_____

_____

_____

My water intake

Notes

_____

_____

_____

_____

_____

| Remember | Breakfast | Lunch | Dinner |

Date: _____

Today I am grateful for

_____

_____

_____

To Do List

☐

☐

☐

☐

Chores

_____

_____

_____

_____

My water intake

Notes

_____

_____

_____

_____

_____

Remember	Breakfast	Lunch	Dinner

Date: _____

Today I am grateful for

_____
_____
_____

To Do List

☐
☐
☐
☐

Chores

_____
_____
_____
_____

My water intake

Notes

_____
_____
_____
_____
_____
_____

| Remember | Breakfast | Lunch | Dinner |

Date: _____

Today I am grateful for

_____
_____

To Do List

☐
☐
☐
☐

Chores

_____
_____
_____
_____

My water intake

Notes

_____
_____
_____
_____
_____

Remember	Breakfast	Lunch	Dinner

Date: _____

Today I am grateful for

_____

_____

To Do List

☐
☐
☐
☐

Chores

_____
_____
_____
_____

My water intake

Notes

_____
_____
_____
_____
_____

| Remember | Breakfast | Lunch | Dinner |

Date: _____

Today I am grateful for

_____
_____

To Do List

☐
☐
☐
☐

Chores

_____
_____
_____
_____

My water intake

Notes

_____
_____
_____
_____
_____

| Remember | Breakfast | Lunch | Dinner |

Date: _____

Today I am grateful for

_____

_____

_____

To Do List

☐

☐

☐

☐

Chores

_____
_____
_____
_____

My water intake

Notes

_____

_____

_____

_____

Remember	Breakfast	Lunch	Dinner

Date: _____

Today I am grateful for

_____
_____
_____

To Do List

- ☐
- ☐
- ☐
- ☐

Chores

_____
_____
_____
_____

My water intake

Notes

_____
_____
_____
_____
_____

Remember	Breakfast	Lunch	Dinner

Date: _____

Today I am grateful for

_____

_____

_____

To Do List

☐
☐
☐
☐

Chores

_____
_____
_____
_____

My water intake

Notes

_____
_____
_____
_____
_____
_____

Remember	Breakfast	Lunch	Dinner

Date: _____

Today I am grateful for

_____
_____
_____

To Do List

☐
☐
☐
☐

Chores

_____
_____
_____

My water intake

Notes

_____
_____
_____
_____
_____
_____

Remember	Breakfast	Lunch	Dinner

Date: _____

Today I am grateful for

_____

_____

_____

To Do List

☐
☐
☐
☐

Chores

_____

_____

_____

My water intake

Notes

_____

_____

_____

_____

_____

| Remember | Breakfast | Lunch | Dinner |

Date: _____

Today I am grateful for

_____

_____

To Do List

☐

☐

☐

☐

Chores

_____

_____

_____

My water intake

Notes

_____

_____

_____

_____

_____

| Remember | Breakfast | Lunch | Dinner |

Date: _____

Today I am grateful for

_____

_____

To Do List

- ☐
- ☐
- ☐
- ☐

Chores

_____

_____

_____

_____

My water intake

Notes

_____

_____

_____

_____

Remember	Breakfast	Lunch	Dinner

Date: _____

Today I am grateful for

_____

_____

_____

To Do List

- [ ]
- [ ]
- [ ]
- [ ]

Chores

_____

_____

_____

_____

My water intake

Notes

_____

_____

_____

_____

_____

Remember	Breakfast	Lunch	Dinner

Date: _____

Today I am grateful for

_____

_____

_____

To Do List

☐

☐

☐

☐

Chores

_____

_____

_____

_____

My water intake

Notes

_____

_____

_____

_____

_____

Remember	Breakfast	Lunch	Dinner

Date: _____

Today I am grateful for

_____

_____

To Do List

☐
☐
☐
☐

Chores

_____
_____
_____

My water intake

Notes

_____
_____
_____
_____
_____

Remember | Breakfast | Lunch | Dinner

Date: _____

Today I am grateful for

_____

_____

_____

To Do List

☐
☐
☐
☐

Chores

_____
_____
_____
_____

My water intake

Notes

_____
_____
_____
_____

Remember	Breakfast	Lunch	Dinner

Date: _____

Today I am grateful for

_____

_____

To Do List

☐

☐

☐

☐

Chores

_____

_____

_____

My water intake

Notes

_____

_____

_____

_____

_____

Remember	Breakfast	Lunch	Dinner

Date: _____

Today I am grateful for

_____
_____
_____

To Do List

☐
☐
☐
☐

Chores

_____
_____
_____
_____

My water intake

Notes

_____
_____
_____
_____
_____

Remember	Breakfast	Lunch	Dinner

Date: _____

Today I am grateful for

_____

_____

_____

To Do List

☐

☐

☐

☐

Chores

_____

_____

_____

_____

My water intake

Notes

_____

_____

_____

_____

_____

| Remember | Breakfast | Lunch | Dinner |

Date: _____

Today I am grateful for

_____

_____

To Do List

- ☐
- ☐
- ☐
- ☐

Chores

_____

_____

_____

_____

My water intake

Notes

_____

_____

_____

_____

_____

Remember	Breakfast	Lunch	Dinner

Date: _____

Today I am grateful for

_____

_____

To Do List

☐
☐
☐
☐

Chores

_____
_____
_____
_____

My water intake

Notes

_____
_____
_____
_____

Remember	Breakfast	Lunch	Dinner

Date: _____

Today I am grateful for

_____

_____

To Do List

☐
☐
☐
☐

Chores

_____
_____
_____
_____

My water intake

Notes

_____
_____
_____
_____
_____

Remember	Breakfast	Lunch	Dinner

Date: _____

Today I am grateful for

_____

_____

To Do List

☐

☐

☐

☐

Chores

_____

_____

_____

_____

My water intake

Notes

_____

_____

_____

_____

_____

| Remember | Breakfast | Lunch | Dinner |

Date: _____

Today I am grateful for

_____

_____

To Do List

☐

☐

☐

☐

Chores

_____

_____

_____

_____

My water intake

Notes

_____

_____

_____

_____

| Remember | Breakfast | Lunch | Dinner |

Date: _____

Today I am grateful for

_____

_____

_____

To Do List

☐
☐
☐
☐

Chores

_____
_____
_____
_____

My water intake

Notes

_____
_____
_____
_____
_____

Remember	Breakfast	Lunch	Dinner

Date: _____

Today I am grateful for

_____

_____

_____

To Do List

☐

☐

☐

☐

Chores

_____

_____

_____

_____

My water intake

Notes

_____

_____

_____

_____

_____

| Remember | Breakfast | Lunch | Dinner |

Date: _____

Today I am grateful for

_____

_____

To Do List

☐

☐

☐

☐

Chores

_____

_____

_____

My water intake

Notes

_____

_____

_____

_____

| Remember | Breakfast | Lunch | Dinner |

Date: _____

Today I am grateful for

_____

_____

_____

To Do List

☐

☐

☐

☐

Chores

_____

_____

_____

_____

My water intake

Notes

_____

_____

_____

_____

_____

Remember	Breakfast	Lunch	Dinner

Date: _____

Today I am grateful for

_____

_____

To Do List

☐
☐
☐
☐

Chores

_____
_____
_____
_____

My water intake

Notes

_____
_____
_____
_____
_____

| Remember | Breakfast | Lunch | Dinner |

Date: _____

Today I am grateful for

_____

_____

_____

To Do List

☐
☐
☐
☐

Chores

_____
_____
_____
_____

My water intake

Notes

_____
_____
_____
_____
_____

| Remember | Breakfast | Lunch | Dinner |

Date: _____

Today I am grateful for

_____

_____

To Do List

☐

☐

☐

☐

Chores

_____

_____

_____

_____

My water intake

Notes

_____

_____

_____

_____

_____

| Remember | Breakfast | Lunch | Dinner |

Date: _____

Today I am grateful for

_____

_____

To Do List

- ☐
- ☐
- ☐
- ☐

Chores

_____

_____

_____

_____

My water intake

Notes

_____

_____

_____

_____

_____

Remember	Breakfast	Lunch	Dinner

Date: _____

Today I am grateful for

_____

_____

To Do List

☐

☐

☐

☐

Chores

_____

_____

_____

My water intake

Notes

_____

_____

_____

_____

_____

| Remember | Breakfast | Lunch | Dinner |

Date: _____

Today I am grateful for

_____
_____
_____

To Do List

☐
☐
☐
☐

Chores

_____
_____
_____
_____

My water intake

Notes

_____
_____
_____
_____
_____

Remember	Breakfast	Lunch	Dinner

Date: _____

Today I am grateful for

_____

_____

To Do List

- ☐
- ☐
- ☐
- ☐

Chores

_____

_____

_____

_____

My water intake

Notes

_____

_____

_____

_____

| Remember | Breakfast | Lunch | Dinner |

Date: _____

Today I am grateful for

_____

_____

To Do List

☐

☐

☐

☐

Chores

_____

_____

_____

_____

My water intake

Notes

_____

_____

_____

_____

_____

Remember	Breakfast	Lunch	Dinner

Date: _____

Today I am grateful for

_____

_____

To Do List

☐

☐

☐

☐

Chores

_____

_____

_____

_____

My water intake

Notes

_____

_____

_____

_____

_____

Remember	Breakfast	Lunch	Dinner

Date: _____

Today I am grateful for

_____

_____

To Do List

☐

☐

☐

☐

Chores

_____

_____

_____

_____

My water intake

Notes

_____

_____

_____

_____

_____

Remember	Breakfast	Lunch	Dinner

Date: _____

Today I am grateful for

_____

_____

_____

To Do List

☐

☐

☐

☐

Chores

_____

_____

_____

My water intake

Notes

_____

_____

_____

_____

_____

Remember	Breakfast	Lunch	Dinner

Date: _____

Today I am grateful for

_____
_____

To Do List

☐
☐
☐
☐

Chores

_____
_____
_____
_____

My water intake

Notes

_____
_____
_____
_____
_____

Remember	Breakfast	Lunch	Dinner

Date: _____

Today I am grateful for

_____

_____

To Do List

☐
☐
☐
☐

Chores

_____
_____
_____
_____

My water intake

Notes

_____
_____
_____
_____
_____

| Remember | Breakfast | Lunch | Dinner |

Date: _____

Today I am grateful for

_____

_____

_____

To Do List

☐

☐

☐

☐

Chores

_____

_____

_____

_____

My water intake

Notes

_____

_____

_____

_____

_____

_____

Remember	Breakfast	Lunch	Dinner

Date: _____

Today I am grateful for

_____
_____
_____

To Do List

☐
☐
☐
☐

Chores

_____
_____
_____
_____

My water intake

Notes

_____
_____
_____
_____
_____

Remember	Breakfast	Lunch	Dinner

Date: _____

Today I am grateful for

_____
_____
_____

To Do List

- [ ]
- [ ]
- [ ]
- [ ]

Chores

_____
_____
_____
_____

My water intake

Notes

_____
_____
_____
_____
_____

| Remember | Breakfast | Lunch | Dinner |

Date: _____

Today I am grateful for

_____

_____

_____

To Do List

☐

☐

☐

☐

Chores

_____

_____

_____

_____

My water intake

Notes

_____

_____

_____

_____

_____

Remember	Breakfast	Lunch	Dinner

Date: _____

Today I am grateful for

_____

_____

To Do List

☐

☐

☐

☐

Chores

_____

_____

_____

_____

My water intake

Notes

_____

_____

_____

_____

_____

Remember	Breakfast	Lunch	Dinner

Date: _____

Today I am grateful for

_____

_____

To Do List

- ☐
- ☐
- ☐
- ☐

Chores

_____

_____

_____

_____

My water intake

Notes

_____

_____

_____

_____

_____

Remember	Breakfast	Lunch	Dinner

Date: _____

Today I am grateful for

_____

_____

To Do List

☐
☐
☐
☐

Chores

_____
_____
_____
_____

My water intake

Notes

_____
_____
_____
_____

Remember	Breakfast	Lunch	Dinner

Date: _____

Today I am grateful for

_____

_____

To Do List

☐

☐

☐

☐

Chores

_____

_____

_____

_____

My water intake

Notes

_____

_____

_____

_____

_____

| Remember | Breakfast | Lunch | Dinner |

Date: _____

Today I am grateful for

_____

_____

To Do List

☐

☐

☐

☐

Chores

_____

_____

_____

_____

My water intake

Notes

_____

_____

_____

_____

_____

| Remember | Breakfast | Lunch | Dinner |

Date: _____

Today I am grateful for

_____

_____

To Do List

☐
☐
☐
☐

Chores

_____

_____

_____

My water intake

Notes

_____

_____

_____

_____

| Remember | Breakfast | Lunch | Dinner |

Date: _____

Today I am grateful for

_____

_____

_____

To Do List

☐
☐
☐
☐

Chores

_____
_____
_____
_____

My water intake

Notes

_____
_____
_____
_____
_____

| Remember | Breakfast | Lunch | Dinner |

Date: _____

Today I am grateful for

_____

_____

To Do List

☐
☐
☐
☐

Chores

_____
_____
_____
_____

My water intake

Notes

_____
_____
_____
_____
_____

| Remember | Breakfast | Lunch | Dinner |

Date: _____

Today I am grateful for

_____

_____

To Do List

☐
☐
☐
☐

Chores

_____
_____
_____
_____

My water intake

Notes

_____
_____
_____
_____
_____

| Remember | Breakfast | Lunch | Dinner |

Date: _____

Today I am grateful for

_____

_____

To Do List

☐

☐

☐

☐

Chores

_____

_____

_____

_____

My water intake

Notes

_____

_____

_____

_____

| Remember | Breakfast | Lunch | Dinner |

Date: _____

Today I am grateful for

_____
_____

To Do List

☐
☐
☐
☐

Chores

_____
_____
_____
_____

My water intake

Notes

_____
_____
_____
_____
_____
_____

Remember | Breakfast | Lunch | Dinner

Date: _____

Today I am grateful for

_____

_____

To Do List

☐

☐

☐

☐

Chores

_____

_____

_____

_____

My water intake

Notes

_____

_____

_____

_____

Remember	Breakfast	Lunch	Dinner

Date: _____

Today I am grateful for

_____
_____
_____

To Do List

☐
☐
☐
☐

Chores

_____
_____
_____
_____

My water intake

Notes

_____
_____
_____
_____
_____

| Remember | Breakfast | Lunch | Dinner |

Date: _____

Today I am grateful for

_____

_____

To Do List

☐
☐
☐
☐

Chores

_____
_____
_____

My water intake

Notes

_____
_____
_____
_____
_____

Remember	Breakfast	Lunch	Dinner

Date: _____

Today I am grateful for

_____

_____

_____

To Do List

☐

☐

☐

☐

Chores

_____

_____

_____

_____

My water intake

Notes

_____

_____

_____

_____

_____

| Remember | Breakfast | Lunch | Dinner |

Date: _____

Today I am grateful for

_____

_____

_____

To Do List

- [ ]
- [ ]
- [ ]
- [ ]

Chores

_____
_____
_____
_____

My water intake

Notes

_____
_____
_____
_____
_____

Remember	Breakfast	Lunch	Dinner

Date: _____

Today I am grateful for

_____

_____

To Do List

☐
☐
☐
☐

Chores

_____
_____
_____
_____

My water intake

Notes

_____
_____
_____
_____
_____

Remember	Breakfast	Lunch	Dinner

Date: _____

Today I am grateful for

_____

_____

_____

To Do List

- [ ]
- [ ]
- [ ]
- [ ]

Chores

_____

_____

_____

My water intake

Notes

_____

_____

_____

_____

_____

Remember	Breakfast	Lunch	Dinner

Date: _____

Today I am grateful for

_____

_____

To Do List

☐

☐

☐

☐

Chores

_____

_____

_____

_____

My water intake

Notes

_____

_____

_____

_____

| Remember | Breakfast | Lunch | Dinner |

Date: _____

Today I am grateful for

_____

_____

To Do List

- [ ]
- [ ]
- [ ]
- [ ]

Chores

_____

_____

_____

My water intake

Notes

_____

_____

_____

_____

_____

Remember	Breakfast	Lunch	Dinner

Date: _____

Today I am grateful for

_____
_____
_____

To Do List

- [ ]
- [ ]
- [ ]
- [ ]

Chores

_____
_____
_____
_____

My water intake

Notes

_____
_____
_____
_____
_____

Remember	Breakfast	Lunch	Dinner

Date: _____

Today I am grateful for

_____

_____

To Do List

☐

☐

☐

☐

Chores

_____

_____

_____

_____

My water intake

Notes

_____

_____

_____

_____

_____

Remember	Breakfast	Lunch	Dinner

Date: _____

Today I am grateful for

_____
_____
_____

To Do List

☐
☐
☐
☐

Chores

_____
_____
_____
_____

My water intake

Notes

_____
_____
_____
_____
_____
_____

| Remember | Breakfast | Lunch | Dinner |

Date: _____

Today I am grateful for

_____
_____
_____

To Do List

☐
☐
☐
☐

Chores
_____
_____
_____
_____

My water intake

Notes

_____
_____
_____
_____
_____

Remember | Breakfast | Lunch | Dinner

Date: _____

Today I am grateful for

_____

_____

To Do List

☐
☐
☐
☐

Chores

_____
_____
_____
_____

My water intake

Notes

_____
_____
_____
_____
_____
_____

| Remember | Breakfast | Lunch | Dinner |

Date: _____

Today I am grateful for

_____

_____

To Do List

☐
☐
☐
☐

Chores

_____
_____
_____

My water intake

Notes

_____
_____
_____
_____
_____

Remember | **Breakfast** | **Lunch** | **Dinner**

Date: _____

Today I am grateful for

_____

_____

To Do List

☐
☐
☐
☐

Chores

_____
_____
_____
_____

My water intake

Notes

_____
_____
_____
_____
_____

| Remember | Breakfast | Lunch | Dinner |

Date: _____

Today I am grateful for

_____

_____

To Do List

- ☐
- ☐
- ☐
- ☐

Chores

_____

_____

_____

_____

My water intake

Notes

_____

_____

_____

_____

_____

Remember	Breakfast	Lunch	Dinner

Date: _____

Today I am grateful for

_____

_____

To Do List

☐
☐
☐
☐

Chores

_____
_____
_____
_____

My water intake

Notes

_____
_____
_____
_____
_____

Remember	Breakfast	Lunch	Dinner

Date: _____

Today I am grateful for

_____

_____

To Do List

☐

☐

☐

☐

Chores

_____

_____

_____

_____

My water intake

Notes

_____

_____

_____

_____

Remember	Breakfast	Lunch	Dinner

Date: _____

Today I am grateful for

_____
_____
_____

To Do List

☐
☐
☐
☐

Chores

_____
_____
_____
_____

My water intake

Notes

_____
_____
_____
_____
_____

| Remember | Breakfast | Lunch | Dinner |

Date: _____

Today I am grateful for

_____

_____

To Do List

☐

☐

☐

☐

Chores

_____

_____

_____

My water intake

Notes

_____

_____

_____

_____

_____

| Remember | Breakfast | Lunch | Dinner |

Date: _____

Today I am grateful for

_____

_____

To Do List

☐
☐
☐
☐

Chores

_____
_____
_____
_____

My water intake

Notes

_____

_____

_____

_____

| Remember | Breakfast | Lunch | Dinner |

Date: _____

Today I am grateful for

_____

_____

To Do List

☐
☐
☐
☐

Chores

_____
_____
_____
_____

My water intake

Notes

_____
_____
_____
_____
_____

Remember	Breakfast	Lunch	Dinner

Date: _____

Today I am grateful for

_____

_____

_____

To Do List

- ☐
- ☐
- ☐
- ☐

Chores

_____

_____

_____

_____

My water intake

Notes

_____

_____

_____

_____

_____

| Remember | Breakfast | Lunch | Dinner |

Date: _____

Today I am grateful for

_____

_____

To Do List

☐

☐

☐

☐

Chores

_____
_____
_____
_____

My water intake

Notes

_____

_____

_____

_____

_____

| Remember | Breakfast | Lunch | Dinner |

Date: _____

Today I am grateful for

_____

_____

_____

To Do List

☐

☐

☐

☐

Chores

_____

_____

_____

_____

My water intake

Notes

_____

_____

_____

_____

_____

Remember	Breakfast	Lunch	Dinner

Date: _____

Today I am grateful for

_____

_____

_____

To Do List

☐

☐

☐

☐

Chores

_____

_____

_____

My water intake

Notes

_____

_____

_____

_____

_____

_____

Remember	Breakfast	Lunch	Dinner

Date: _____

Today I am grateful for

_____

_____

To Do List

- ☐
- ☐
- ☐
- ☐

Chores

_____

_____

_____

_____

My water intake

Notes

_____

_____

_____

_____

Remember	Breakfast	Lunch	Dinner

Date: _____

Today I am grateful for

_____

_____

_____

To Do List

☐
☐
☐
☐

Chores

_____

_____

_____

_____

My water intake

Notes

_____

_____

_____

_____

_____

| Remember | Breakfast | Lunch | Dinner |

Date: _____

Today I am grateful for

_____
_____
_____

To Do List

☐
☐
☐
☐

Chores

_____
_____
_____
_____

My water intake

Notes

_____
_____
_____
_____
_____

Remember	Breakfast	Lunch	Dinner

Date: _____

Today I am grateful for

_____

_____

_____

To Do List

- ☐
- ☐
- ☐
- ☐

Chores

_____

_____

_____

_____

My water intake

Notes

_____

_____

_____

_____

_____

Remember	Breakfast	Lunch	Dinner

Date: _____

Today I am grateful for

_____

_____

To Do List

☐
☐
☐
☐

Chores

_____
_____
_____
_____

My water intake

Notes

_____
_____
_____
_____
_____

Remember	Breakfast	Lunch	Dinner

Date: _____

Today I am grateful for

_____

_____

_____

To Do List

☐

☐

☐

☐

Chores

_____

_____

_____

My water intake

Notes

_____

_____

_____

_____

_____

Remember	Breakfast	Lunch	Dinner

Date: _____

Today I am grateful for

_____
_____

To Do List

☐
☐
☐
☐

Chores

_____
_____
_____
_____

My water intake

Notes

_____
_____
_____
_____
_____

Remember	Breakfast	Lunch	Dinner

Date: _____

Today I am grateful for

_____

_____

_____

To Do List

☐
☐
☐
☐

Chores

_____
_____
_____
_____

My water intake

Notes

_____
_____
_____
_____
_____

| Remember | Breakfast | Lunch | Dinner |

Date: _____

Today I am grateful for

_____
_____

To Do List

☐
☐
☐
☐

Chores
_____
_____
_____
_____

My water intake

Notes

_____
_____
_____
_____
_____

| Remember | Breakfast | Lunch | Dinner |

Date: _____

Today I am grateful for

_____

_____

_____

To Do List

☐
☐
☐
☐

Chores

_____
_____
_____
_____

My water intake

Notes

_____
_____
_____
_____
_____

Remember	Breakfast	Lunch	Dinner

Date: _____

Today I am grateful for

_____

_____

To Do List

☐

☐

☐

☐

Chores

_____

_____

_____

_____

My water intake

Notes

_____

_____

_____

_____

_____

_____

Remember	Breakfast	Lunch	Dinner

Date: _____

Today I am grateful for

_____

_____

To Do List

☐

☐

☐

☐

Chores

_____

_____

_____

My water intake

Notes

_____

_____

_____

_____

_____

| Remember | Breakfast | Lunch | Dinner |

Date: _____

Today I am grateful for

_____
_____

To Do List

☐
☐
☐
☐

Chores

_____
_____
_____
_____

My water intake

Notes

_____
_____
_____
_____
_____

| Remember | Breakfast | Lunch | Dinner |

Date: _____

Today I am grateful for

_____

_____

_____

To Do List

☐

☐

☐

☐

Chores

_____

_____

_____

_____

My water intake

Notes

_____

_____

_____

_____

_____

Remember	Breakfast	Lunch	Dinner

Date: _____

Today I am grateful for

_____
_____
_____

To Do List

☐
☐
☐
☐

Chores

_____
_____
_____
_____
_____

My water intake

Notes

_____
_____
_____
_____
_____

Remember	Breakfast	Lunch	Dinner

Date: _____

Today I am grateful for

_____

_____

To Do List

☐

☐

☐

☐

Chores

_____

_____

_____

My water intake

Notes

_____

_____

_____

_____

_____

Remember	Breakfast	Lunch	Dinner

Date: _____

Today I am grateful for

_____

_____

_____

To Do List

☐

☐

☐

☐

Chores

_____

_____

_____

_____

My water intake

Notes

_____

_____

_____

_____

_____

_____

Remember	Breakfast	Lunch	Dinner

Date: _____

Today I am grateful for

_____

_____

_____

To Do List

☐

☐

☐

☐

Chores

_____

_____

_____

My water intake

Notes

_____

_____

_____

_____

_____

| Remember | Breakfast | Lunch | Dinner |

Date: _____

Today I am grateful for

_____

_____

To Do List

☐

☐

☐

☐

Chores

_____

_____

_____

_____

My water intake

Notes

_____

_____

_____

_____

_____

| Remember | Breakfast | Lunch | Dinner |

Date: _____

Today I am grateful for

_____

_____

_____

To Do List

☐

☐

☐

☐

Chores

_____

_____

_____

_____

My water intake

Notes

_____

_____

_____

_____

_____

Remember	Breakfast	Lunch	Dinner

Date: _____

Today I am grateful for

_____

_____

To Do List

☐

☐

☐

☐

Chores

_____

_____

_____

_____

My water intake

Notes

_____

_____

_____

_____

_____

Remember	Breakfast	Lunch	Dinner

Date: _____

Today I am grateful for

_____

_____

_____

To Do List

☐

☐

☐

☐

Chores

_____

_____

_____

_____

My water intake

Notes

_____

_____

_____

_____

_____

Remember	Breakfast	Lunch	Dinner

Date: _____

Today I am grateful for

_____
_____
_____

To Do List

☐
☐
☐
☐

Chores

_____
_____
_____
_____

My water intake

Notes

_____
_____
_____
_____
_____
_____

| Remember | Breakfast | Lunch | Dinner |

Date: _____

Today I am grateful for

_____

_____

To Do List

- ☐
- ☐
- ☐
- ☐

Chores

_____

_____

_____

_____

My water intake

Notes

_____

_____

_____

_____

Remember	Breakfast	Lunch	Dinner

Date: _____

Today I am grateful for

_____

_____

_____

To Do List

☐

☐

☐

☐

Chores

_____

_____

_____

_____

My water intake

Notes

_____

_____

_____

_____

Remember	Breakfast	Lunch	Dinner

Date: _____

Today I am grateful for

_____

_____

_____

To Do List

☐

☐

☐

☐

Chores

_____

_____

_____

My water intake

Notes

_____

_____

_____

_____

Remember	Breakfast	Lunch	Dinner

Date: _____

Today I am grateful for

_____

_____

_____

To Do List

☐

☐

☐

☐

Chores

_____

_____

_____

_____

My water intake

Notes

_____

_____

_____

_____

_____

| Remember | Breakfast | Lunch | Dinner |

Date: _____

Today I am grateful for

_____

_____

To Do List

☐

☐

☐

☐

Chores

_____

_____

_____

_____

My water intake

Notes

_____

_____

_____

_____

Remember	Breakfast	Lunch	Dinner

Date: _____

Today I am grateful for

_____
_____
_____

To Do List

☐
☐
☐
☐

Chores

_____
_____
_____
_____

My water intake

Notes

_____
_____
_____
_____
_____

Remember	Breakfast	Lunch	Dinner

Date: _____

Today I am grateful for

_____

_____

_____

To Do List

☐

☐

☐

☐

Chores

_____

_____

_____

_____

My water intake

Notes

_____

_____

_____

_____

_____

Remember	Breakfast	Lunch	Dinner

Date: _____

Today I am grateful for

_____
_____
_____

To Do List

☐
☐
☐
☐

Chores

_____
_____
_____
_____

My water intake

Notes

_____
_____
_____
_____
_____

Remember	Breakfast	Lunch	Dinner

Date: _____

Today I am grateful for

_____

_____

_____

To Do List

☐
☐
☐
☐

Chores

_____
_____
_____
_____

My water intake

Notes

_____
_____
_____
_____
_____

| Remember | Breakfast | Lunch | Dinner |

Date: _____

Today I am grateful for

_____

_____

To Do List

☐
☐
☐
☐

Chores

_____
_____
_____
_____

My water intake

Notes

_____
_____
_____
_____
_____
_____

| Remember | Breakfast | Lunch | Dinner |

Date: _____

Today I am grateful for

_____

_____

To Do List

- ☐
- ☐
- ☐
- ☐

Chores

_____
_____
_____
_____

My water intake

Notes

_____
_____
_____
_____
_____

| Remember | Breakfast | Lunch | Dinner |

Date: _____

Today I am grateful for

_____

_____

To Do List

☐
☐
☐
☐

Chores

_____
_____
_____
_____
_____

My water intake

Notes

_____
_____
_____
_____
_____

Remember	Breakfast	Lunch	Dinner

Date: _____

Today I am grateful for

_____

_____

To Do List

☐
☐
☐
☐

Chores

_____
_____
_____
_____

My water intake

Notes

_____
_____
_____
_____
_____

Remember	Breakfast	Lunch	Dinner

Date: _____

Today I am grateful for

_____

_____

To Do List

☐

☐

☐

☐

Chores

_____

_____

_____

_____

My water intake

Notes

_____

_____

_____

_____

Remember	Breakfast	Lunch	Dinner

Date: _____

Today I am grateful for

_____

_____

To Do List

☐

☐

☐

☐

Chores

_____

_____

_____

_____

My water intake

Notes

_____

_____

_____

_____

_____

Remember	Breakfast	Lunch	Dinner

Date: _____

Today I am grateful for

_____
_____

To Do List

☐
☐
☐
☐

Chores

_____
_____
_____

My water intake

Notes

_____
_____
_____
_____
_____

Remember	Breakfast	Lunch	Dinner

Date: _____

Today I am grateful for

_____

_____

_____

To Do List

- [ ]
- [ ]
- [ ]
- [ ]

Chores

_____

_____

_____

My water intake

Notes

_____

_____

_____

_____

_____

Remember	Breakfast	Lunch	Dinner

Date: _____

Today I am grateful for

_____

_____

_____

To Do List

☐

☐

☐

☐

Chores

_____

_____

_____

_____

My water intake

Notes

_____

_____

_____

_____

| Remember | Breakfast | Lunch | Dinner |

Date: _____

Today I am grateful for

_____

_____

To Do List

☐

☐

☐

☐

Chores

_____

_____

_____

My water intake

Notes

_____

_____

_____

_____

_____

| Remember | Breakfast | Lunch | Dinner |

Date: _____

Today I am grateful for

_____

_____

_____

To Do List

☐

☐

☐

☐

Chores

_____

_____

_____

_____

My water intake

Notes

_____

_____

_____

_____

_____

Remember	Breakfast	Lunch	Dinner

Date: _____

Today I am grateful for

_____

_____

_____

To Do List

☐

☐

☐

☐

Chores

_____

_____

_____

_____

My water intake

Notes

_____

_____

_____

_____

_____

| Remember | Breakfast | Lunch | Dinner |

Date: _____

Today I am grateful for

_____

_____

To Do List

☐

☐

☐

☐

Chores

_____

_____

_____

_____

My water intake

Notes

_____

_____

_____

_____

_____

Remember	Breakfast	Lunch	Dinner

Date: _____

Today I am grateful for

_____
_____
_____

To Do List

☐
☐
☐
☐

Chores

_____
_____
_____
_____

My water intake

Notes

_____
_____
_____
_____
_____

Remember	Breakfast	Lunch	Dinner

Date: _____

Today I am grateful for

_____

_____

To Do List

☐

☐

☐

☐

Chores

_____

_____

_____

_____

My water intake

Notes

_____

_____

_____

_____

_____

| Remember | Breakfast | Lunch | Dinner |

Date: _____

Today I am grateful for

_____

_____

_____

To Do List

☐
☐
☐
☐

Chores

_____
_____
_____

My water intake

Notes

_____
_____
_____
_____
_____

| Remember | Breakfast | Lunch | Dinner |

Date: _____

Today I am grateful for

_____

_____

To Do List

☐
☐
☐
☐

Chores

_____
_____
_____
_____

My water intake

Notes

_____

_____

_____

_____

_____

| Remember | Breakfast | Lunch | Dinner |

Date: _____

Today I am grateful for

_____

_____

_____

To Do List

☐

☐

☐

☐

Chores

_____

_____

_____

_____

My water intake

Notes

_____

_____

_____

_____

Remember	Breakfast	Lunch	Dinner

Date: _____

Today I am grateful for

_____

_____

_____

To Do List

☐

☐

☐

☐

Chores

_____

_____

_____

_____

My water intake

Notes

_____

_____

_____

_____

_____

| Remember | Breakfast | Lunch | Dinner |

Date: _____

Today I am grateful for

_____

_____

_____

To Do List

☐

☐

☐

☐

Chores

_____

_____

_____

_____

My water intake

Notes

_____

_____

_____

_____

_____

Remember	Breakfast	Lunch	Dinner

Date: _____

Today I am grateful for

_____

_____

To Do List

☐

☐

☐

☐

Chores

_____

_____

_____

_____

My water intake

Notes

_____

_____

_____

_____

_____

Remember	Breakfast	Lunch	Dinner

Date: _____

Today I am grateful for

_____

_____

_____

To Do List

☐
☐
☐
☐

Chores

_____
_____
_____
_____

My water intake

Notes

_____
_____
_____
_____
_____

| Remember | Breakfast | Lunch | Dinner |

Date: _____

Today I am grateful for

_____
_____
_____

To Do List

☐
☐
☐
☐

Chores

_____
_____
_____
_____

My water intake

Notes

_____
_____
_____
_____
_____

| Remember | Breakfast | Lunch | Dinner |

Date: _____

Today I am grateful for

_____

_____

_____

To Do List

☐

☐

☐

☐

Chores

_____

_____

_____

_____

My water intake

Notes

_____

_____

_____

_____

_____

Remember	Breakfast	Lunch	Dinner

Date: _____

Today I am grateful for

_____

_____

To Do List

☐

☐

☐

☐

Chores

_____

_____

_____

_____

My water intake

Notes

_____

_____

_____

_____

_____

Remember	Breakfast	Lunch	Dinner

Date: _____

Today I am grateful for

_____

_____

To Do List

- [ ]
- [ ]
- [ ]
- [ ]

Chores

_____
_____
_____
_____

My water intake

Notes

_____
_____
_____
_____
_____
_____

Remember	Breakfast	Lunch	Dinner

Date: _____

Today I am grateful for

_____

_____

To Do List

☐

☐

☐

☐

Chores

_____

_____

_____

_____

My water intake

Notes

_____

_____

_____

_____

_____

Remember	Breakfast	Lunch	Dinner

Date: _____

Today I am grateful for

_____

_____

To Do List

☐

☐

☐

☐

Chores

_____

_____

_____

My water intake

Notes

_____

_____

_____

_____

Remember	Breakfast	Lunch	Dinner

Date: _____

Today I am grateful for

_____

_____

To Do List

☐
☐
☐
☐

Chores

_____
_____
_____
_____

My water intake

Notes

_____

_____

_____

_____

_____

Remember	Breakfast	Lunch	Dinner

Date: _____

Today I am grateful for

_____

_____

To Do List

☐

☐

☐

☐

Chores

_____

_____

_____

_____

My water intake

Notes

_____

_____

_____

_____

_____

Remember	Breakfast	Lunch	Dinner

Date: _____

Today I am grateful for

_____

_____

_____

To Do List

☐
☐
☐
☐

Chores

_____

_____

_____

_____

My water intake

Notes

_____

_____

_____

_____

_____

Remember	Breakfast	Lunch	Dinner

Date: _____

Today I am grateful for

_____
_____
_____

To Do List

☐
☐
☐
☐

Chores

_____
_____
_____
_____

My water intake

Notes

_____
_____
_____
_____
_____

| Remember | Breakfast | Lunch | Dinner |

Date: _____

Today I am grateful for

_____
_____
_____

To Do List

☐
☐
☐
☐

Chores

_____
_____
_____
_____

My water intake

Notes

_____
_____
_____
_____
_____

| Remember | Breakfast | Lunch | Dinner |

Date: _____

Today I am grateful for

_____

_____

_____

To Do List

☐

☐

☐

☐

Chores

_____

_____

_____

My water intake

Notes

_____

_____

_____

_____

_____

| Remember | Breakfast | Lunch | Dinner |

Date: _____

Today I am grateful for

_____

_____

To Do List

☐

☐

☐

☐

Chores

_____

_____

_____

_____

My water intake

Notes

_____

_____

_____

_____

| Remember | Breakfast | Lunch | Dinner |

Date: _____

Today I am grateful for

_____
_____
_____

To Do List

☐
☐
☐
☐

Chores

_____
_____
_____

My water intake

Notes

_____
_____
_____
_____
_____

Remember	Breakfast	Lunch	Dinner

Date: _____

Today I am grateful for

_____

_____

_____

To Do List

☐

☐

☐

☐

Chores

_____

_____

_____

_____

My water intake

Notes

_____

_____

_____

_____

_____

Remember	Breakfast	Lunch	Dinner

Date: _____

Today I am grateful for

_____

_____

_____

To Do List

☐

☐

☐

☐

Chores

_____

_____

_____

_____

My water intake

Notes

_____

_____

_____

_____

_____

Remember	Breakfast	Lunch	Dinner

Date: _____

Today I am grateful for

_____
_____
_____

To Do List

☐
☐
☐
☐

Chores

_____
_____
_____
_____

My water intake

Notes

_____
_____
_____
_____
_____

Remember	Breakfast	Lunch	Dinner

Date: _____

Today I am grateful for

_____

_____

_____

To Do List

☐
☐
☐
☐

Chores

_____
_____
_____
_____

My water intake

Notes

_____
_____
_____
_____
_____

Remember	Breakfast	Lunch	Dinner

Date: _____

Today I am grateful for

_____

_____

To Do List

☐
☐
☐
☐

Chores

_____
_____
_____
_____

My water intake

Notes

_____
_____
_____
_____
_____

Remember	Breakfast	Lunch	Dinner

Date: _____

Today I am grateful for

_____

_____

To Do List

- ☐
- ☐
- ☐
- ☐

Chores

_____
_____
_____
_____

My water intake

Notes

_____
_____
_____
_____
_____

Remember	Breakfast	Lunch	Dinner

Date: _____

Today I am grateful for

_____

_____

_____

To Do List

☐

☐

☐

☐

Chores

_____

_____

_____

_____

My water intake

Notes

_____

_____

_____

_____

_____

Remember	Breakfast	Lunch	Dinner

Date: _____

Today I am grateful for

_____

_____

_____

To Do List

- ☐
- ☐
- ☐
- ☐

Chores

_____

_____

_____

_____

My water intake

Notes

_____

_____

_____

_____

_____

| Remember | Breakfast | Lunch | Dinner |

Date: _____

Today I am grateful for

_____

_____

To Do List

☐

☐

☐

☐

Chores

_____

_____

_____

_____

My water intake

Notes

_____

_____

_____

_____

| Remember | Breakfast | Lunch | Dinner |

Date: _____

Today I am grateful for

_____

_____

_____

To Do List

- ☐
- ☐
- ☐
- ☐

Chores

_____

_____

_____

_____

My water intake

Notes

_____

_____

_____

_____

_____

Remember	Breakfast	Lunch	Dinner

Date: _____

Today I am grateful for

_____

_____

_____

To Do List

☐

☐

☐

☐

Chores

_____

_____

_____

_____

My water intake

Notes

_____

_____

_____

_____

_____

Remember	Breakfast	Lunch	Dinner

Date: _____

Today I am grateful for

_____

_____

_____

To Do List

☐

☐

☐

☐

Chores

_____

_____

_____

_____

My water intake

Notes

_____

_____

_____

_____

_____

Remember	Breakfast	Lunch	Dinner

Date: _____

Today I am grateful for

_____

_____

To Do List

☐

☐

☐

☐

Chores

_____

_____

_____

_____

My water intake

Notes

_____

_____

_____

_____

_____

Remember	Breakfast	Lunch	Dinner

Date: _____

Today I am grateful for

_____

_____

To Do List

- ☐
- ☐
- ☐
- ☐

Chores

_____

_____

_____

My water intake

Notes

_____

_____

_____

_____

_____

Remember	Breakfast	Lunch	Dinner

Date: _____

Today I am grateful for

_____

_____

To Do List

☐
☐
☐
☐

Chores

_____
_____
_____
_____

My water intake

Notes

_____
_____
_____
_____
_____

| Remember | Breakfast | Lunch | Dinner |

Date: _____

Today I am grateful for

_____

_____

To Do List

☐

☐

☐

☐

Chores

_____

_____

_____

_____

My water intake

Notes

_____

_____

_____

_____

_____

| Remember | Breakfast | Lunch | Dinner |

Date: _____

Today I am grateful for

_____

_____

To Do List

☐

☐

☐

☐

Chores

_____

_____

_____

_____

My water intake

Notes

_____

_____

_____

_____

_____

| Remember | Breakfast | Lunch | Dinner |

Date: _____

Today I am grateful for

_____

_____

_____

To Do List

☐

☐

☐

☐

Chores

_____

_____

_____

_____

My water intake

Notes

_____

_____

_____

_____

_____

Remember	Breakfast	Lunch	Dinner

Date: _____

Today I am grateful for

_____

_____

To Do List

☐
☐
☐
☐

Chores

_____
_____
_____
_____

My water intake

Notes

_____
_____
_____
_____
_____

| Remember | Breakfast | Lunch | Dinner |

Date: _____

Today I am grateful for

_____

_____

_____

To Do List

☐
☐
☐
☐

Chores

_____
_____
_____
_____

My water intake

Notes

_____
_____
_____
_____
_____

Remember | Breakfast | Lunch | Dinner

Date: _____

Today I am grateful for

_____

_____

_____

To Do List

☐
☐
☐
☐

Chores

_____
_____
_____
_____

My water intake

Notes

_____

_____

_____

_____

_____

Remember	Breakfast	Lunch	Dinner

Date: _____

Today I am grateful for

_____

_____

To Do List

☐

☐

☐

☐

Chores

_____

_____

_____

My water intake

Notes

_____

_____

_____

_____

_____

| Remember | Breakfast | Lunch | Dinner |

Date: _____

Today I am grateful for

_____

_____

To Do List

☐

☐

☐

☐

Chores

_____

_____

_____

_____

My water intake

Notes

_____

_____

_____

_____

Remember	Breakfast	Lunch	Dinner

Date: _____

Today I am grateful for

_____
_____

To Do List

- [ ]
- [ ]
- [ ]
- [ ]

Chores

_____
_____
_____
_____

My water intake

Notes

_____
_____
_____
_____
_____

Remember	Breakfast	Lunch	Dinner

Date: _____

Today I am grateful for

_____

_____

_____

To Do List

☐
☐
☐
☐

Chores

_____
_____
_____
_____

My water intake

Notes

_____
_____
_____
_____
_____

| Remember | Breakfast | Lunch | Dinner |

Date: _____

Today I am grateful for

_____

_____

To Do List

- ☐
- ☐
- ☐
- ☐

Chores

_____
_____
_____
_____

My water intake

Notes

_____
_____
_____
_____
_____

| Remember | Breakfast | Lunch | Dinner |

Date: _____

Today I am grateful for

_____

_____

_____

To Do List

☐

☐

☐

☐

Chores

_____

_____

_____

_____

My water intake

Notes

_____

_____

_____

_____

_____

| Remember | Breakfast | Lunch | Dinner |

Date: _____

Today I am grateful for

_____

_____

To Do List

☐

☐

☐

☐

Chores

_____

_____

_____

_____

My water intake

Notes

_____

_____

_____

_____

_____

| Remember | Breakfast | Lunch | Dinner |

Date: _____

Today I am grateful for

_____

_____

_____

To Do List

- ☐
- ☐
- ☐
- ☐

Chores

_____

_____

_____

My water intake

Notes

_____

_____

_____

_____

_____

| Remember | Breakfast | Lunch | Dinner |

Date: _____

Today I am grateful for

_____

_____

_____

To Do List

☐

☐

☐

☐

Chores

_____

_____

_____

_____

My water intake

Notes

_____

_____

_____

_____

Remember	Breakfast	Lunch	Dinner

Date: _____

Today I am grateful for

_____
_____
_____

To Do List

☐
☐
☐
☐

Chores

_____
_____
_____
_____

My water intake

Notes

_____
_____
_____
_____
_____

| Remember | Breakfast | Lunch | Dinner |

Date: _____

Today I am grateful for

_____

_____

To Do List

☐

☐

☐

☐

Chores

_____

_____

_____

_____

My water intake

Notes

_____

_____

_____

_____

_____

| Remember | Breakfast | Lunch | Dinner |

Date: _____

Today I am grateful for

_____

_____

_____

To Do List

☐

☐

☐

☐

Chores

_____

_____

_____

_____

My water intake

Notes

_____

_____

_____

_____

_____

_____

Remember	Breakfast	Lunch	Dinner

Date: _____

Today I am grateful for

_____

_____

To Do List

☐

☐

☐

☐

Chores

_____

_____

_____

My water intake

Notes

_____

_____

_____

_____

_____

| Remember | Breakfast | Lunch | Dinner |

Date: _____

Today I am grateful for

_____

_____

To Do List

☐

☐

☐

☐

Chores

_____

_____

_____

_____

My water intake

Notes

_____

_____

_____

_____

_____

Remember	Breakfast	Lunch	Dinner

Date: _____

Today I am grateful for

_____

_____

_____

To Do List

☐

☐

☐

☐

Chores

_____

_____

_____

My water intake

Notes

_____

_____

_____

_____

_____

Remember | Breakfast | Lunch | Dinner

Date: _____

Today I am grateful for

_____

_____

To Do List

☐
☐
☐
☐

Chores

_____
_____
_____
_____

My water intake

Notes

_____
_____
_____
_____
_____

Remember	Breakfast	Lunch	Dinner

Date: _____

Today I am grateful for

_____

_____

To Do List

☐

☐

☐

☐

Chores

_____

_____

_____

_____

My water intake

Notes

_____

_____

_____

_____

_____

Remember	Breakfast	Lunch	Dinner

Date: _____

Today I am grateful for

To Do List

☐
☐
☐
☐

Chores

_____
_____
_____
_____

My water intake

Notes

| Remember | Breakfast | Lunch | Dinner |

Date: _____

Today I am grateful for

_____

_____

_____

To Do List

- ☐
- ☐
- ☐
- ☐

Chores

_____

_____

_____

_____

My water intake

Notes

_____

_____

_____

_____

_____

Remember	Breakfast	Lunch	Dinner

Date: _____

Today I am grateful for

_____

_____

To Do List

☐
☐
☐
☐

Chores

_____
_____
_____
_____

My water intake

Notes

_____

_____

_____

_____

| Remember | Breakfast | Lunch | Dinner |

Date: _____

Today I am grateful for

_____

_____

_____

To Do List

☐

☐

☐

☐

Chores

_____

_____

_____

_____

My water intake

Notes

_____

_____

_____

_____

_____

Remember	Breakfast	Lunch	Dinner

Date: _____

Today I am grateful for

_____

_____

To Do List

☐
☐
☐
☐

Chores

_____
_____
_____
_____

My water intake

Notes

_____
_____
_____
_____
_____

| Remember | Breakfast | Lunch | Dinner |

Date: _____

Today I am grateful for

_____

_____

_____

To Do List

☐

☐

☐

☐

Chores

_____

_____

_____

My water intake

Notes

_____

_____

_____

_____

_____

Remember	Breakfast	Lunch	Dinner

Date: _____

Today I am grateful for

_____

_____

To Do List

☐

☐

☐

☐

Chores

_____

_____

_____

_____

My water intake

Notes

_____

_____

_____

_____

_____

_____

Remember	Breakfast	Lunch	Dinner

Date: _____

Today I am grateful for

_____

_____

To Do List

☐

☐

☐

☐

Chores

_____

_____

_____

_____

My water intake

Notes

_____

_____

_____

_____

Remember	Breakfast	Lunch	Dinner

Date: _____

Today I am grateful for

_____

_____

_____

To Do List

☐

☐

☐

☐

Chores

_____

_____

_____

_____

My water intake

Notes

_____

_____

_____

_____

_____

| Remember | Breakfast | Lunch | Dinner |

Date: _____

Today I am grateful for

_____
_____
_____

To Do List

☐
☐
☐
☐

Chores

_____
_____
_____
_____

My water intake

Notes

_____
_____
_____
_____
_____

| Remember | Breakfast | Lunch | Dinner |

Date: _____

Today I am grateful for

_____

_____

To Do List

☐

☐

☐

☐

Chores

_____

_____

_____

_____

My water intake

Notes

_____

_____

_____

_____

_____

| Remember | Breakfast | Lunch | Dinner |

Date: _____

Today I am grateful for

_____

_____

_____

To Do List

- ☐
- ☐
- ☐
- ☐

Chores

_____
_____
_____
_____

My water intake

Notes

_____
_____
_____
_____
_____

Remember	Breakfast	Lunch	Dinner

Date: _____

Today I am grateful for

_____

_____

_____

To Do List

- ☐
- ☐
- ☐
- ☐

Chores

_____

_____

_____

_____

My water intake

Notes

_____

_____

_____

_____

_____

Remember	Breakfast	Lunch	Dinner

Date: _____

Today I am grateful for

_____

_____

To Do List

☐
☐
☐
☐

Chores

_____
_____
_____

My water intake

Notes

_____
_____
_____
_____
_____

Remember	Breakfast	Lunch	Dinner

Date: _____

Today I am grateful for

_____

_____

To Do List

☐
☐
☐
☐

Chores

_____
_____
_____
_____

My water intake

Notes

_____
_____
_____
_____
_____

Remember	Breakfast	Lunch	Dinner

Date: _____

Today I am grateful for

_____

_____

To Do List

☐

☐

☐

☐

Chores

_____

_____

_____

_____

My water intake

Notes

_____

_____

_____

_____

_____

Remember	Breakfast	Lunch	Dinner

Date: _____

Today I am grateful for

_____

_____

_____

To Do List

☐
☐
☐
☐

Chores

_____
_____
_____
_____

My water intake

Notes

_____
_____
_____
_____
_____

Remember	Breakfast	Lunch	Dinner

Date: _____

Today I am grateful for

_____

_____

To Do List

☐

☐

☐

☐

Chores

_____

_____

_____

_____

My water intake

Notes

_____

_____

_____

_____

_____

| Remember | Breakfast | Lunch | Dinner |

Date: _____

Today I am grateful for

_____

_____

To Do List

- ☐
- ☐
- ☐
- ☐

Chores

_____

_____

_____

_____

My water intake

Notes

_____

_____

_____

_____

_____

Remember	Breakfast	Lunch	Dinner

Date: _____

Today I am grateful for

_____

_____

To Do List

☐

☐

☐

☐

Chores

_____

_____

_____

My water intake

Notes

_____

_____

_____

_____

Remember	Breakfast	Lunch	Dinner

Date: _____

Today I am grateful for

_____
_____

To Do List

☐
☐
☐
☐

Chores

_____
_____
_____
_____

My water intake

Notes

_____
_____
_____
_____

Remember	Breakfast	Lunch	Dinner

Date: _____

Today I am grateful for

_____

_____

_____

To Do List

☐

☐

☐

☐

Chores

_____

_____

_____

_____

My water intake

Notes

_____

_____

_____

_____

_____

Remember	Breakfast	Lunch	Dinner

Date: _____

Today I am grateful for

_____

_____

To Do List

☐
☐
☐
☐

Chores

_____
_____
_____
_____

My water intake

Notes

_____
_____
_____
_____
_____

Remember | Breakfast | Lunch | Dinner

Date: _____

Today I am grateful for

_____

_____

To Do List

☐
☐
☐
☐

Chores

_____
_____
_____
_____

My water intake

Notes

_____
_____
_____
_____
_____

Remember	Breakfast	Lunch	Dinner

Date: _____

Today I am grateful for

_____

_____

To Do List

Chores

- [ ] _____
- [ ] _____
- [ ] _____
- [ ] _____

_____
_____
_____
_____

My water intake

Notes

_____

_____

_____

_____

_____

Remember	Breakfast	Lunch	Dinner

Date: _____

Today I am grateful for

_____

_____

To Do List

- ☐
- ☐
- ☐
- ☐

Chores

_____

_____

_____

My water intake

Notes

_____

_____

_____

_____

_____

Remember	Breakfast	Lunch	Dinner

Date: _____

Today I am grateful for

_____

_____

_____

To Do List

☐
☐
☐
☐

Chores

_____
_____
_____
_____

My water intake

Notes

_____
_____
_____
_____
_____

Remember	Breakfast	Lunch	Dinner

Date: _____

Today I am grateful for

_____

_____

_____

To Do List

☐

☐

☐

☐

Chores

_____

_____

_____

_____

My water intake

Notes

_____

_____

_____

_____

_____

Remember	Breakfast	Lunch	Dinner

Date: _____

Today I am grateful for

_____

_____

_____

To Do List

- ☐
- ☐
- ☐
- ☐

Chores

_____

_____

_____

_____

My water intake

Notes

_____

_____

_____

_____

_____

Remember	Breakfast	Lunch	Dinner

Date: _____

Today I am grateful for

_____

_____

To Do List

☐

☐

☐

☐

Chores

_____

_____

_____

My water intake

Notes

_____

_____

_____

_____

_____

| Remember | Breakfast | Lunch | Dinner |

Date: _____

Today I am grateful for

_____
_____
_____

To Do List

☐
☐
☐
☐

Chores

_____
_____
_____
_____

My water intake

Notes

_____
_____
_____
_____
_____
_____
_____

| Remember | Breakfast | Lunch | Dinner |

Date: _____

Today I am grateful for

_____
_____

To Do List

☐
☐
☐
☐

Chores

_____
_____
_____

My water intake

Notes

_____
_____
_____
_____

Remember

Breakfast

Lunch

Dinner

Date: _____

Today I am grateful for

_____

_____

To Do List

- ☐
- ☐
- ☐
- ☐

Chores

_____

_____

_____

_____

My water intake

Notes

_____

_____

_____

_____

| Remember | Breakfast | Lunch | Dinner |

Date: _____

Today I am grateful for

_____

_____

To Do List

☐

☐

☐

☐

Chores

_____
_____
_____
_____

My water intake

Notes

_____

_____

_____

_____

_____

| Remember | Breakfast | Lunch | Dinner |

Date: _____

Today I am grateful for

_____

_____

_____

To Do List

☐

☐

☐

☐

Chores

_____

_____

_____

_____

My water intake

Notes

_____

_____

_____

_____

_____

Remember	Breakfast	Lunch	Dinner

Date: _____

Today I am grateful for

_____

_____

To Do List

☐
☐
☐
☐

Chores

_____
_____
_____
_____

My water intake

Notes

_____
_____
_____
_____
_____

Remember | Breakfast | Lunch | Dinner

Date: _____

Today I am grateful for

_____

_____

To Do List

☐
☐
☐
☐

Chores

_____
_____
_____
_____

My water intake

Notes

_____
_____
_____
_____
_____

| Remember | Breakfast | Lunch | Dinner |

Date: _____

Today I am grateful for

_____

_____

To Do List

☐
☐
☐
☐

Chores

_____
_____
_____
_____

My water intake

Notes

_____
_____
_____
_____
_____

Remember

Breakfast

Lunch

Dinner

Date: _____

Today I am grateful for

_____
_____

To Do List

☐
☐
☐
☐

Chores
_____
_____
_____
_____

My water intake

Notes

_____
_____
_____
_____
_____

Remember | Breakfast | Lunch | Dinner

Date: _____

Today I am grateful for

_____
_____
_____

To Do List

☐
☐
☐
☐

Chores

_____
_____
_____
_____

My water intake

Notes

_____
_____
_____
_____
_____

Remember	Breakfast	Lunch	Dinner

Date: _____

Today I am grateful for

_____

_____

To Do List

☐
☐
☐
☐

Chores

_____
_____
_____
_____

My water intake

Notes

_____
_____
_____
_____

Remember	Breakfast	Lunch	Dinner

Date: _____

Today I am grateful for

_____
_____
_____

To Do List

☐
☐
☐
☐

Chores

_____
_____
_____
_____

My water intake

Notes

_____
_____
_____
_____
_____

| Remember | Breakfast | Lunch | Dinner |

Date: _____

Today I am grateful for

_____

_____

_____

To Do List

☐

☐

☐

☐

Chores

_____

_____

_____

_____

My water intake

Notes

_____

_____

_____

_____

_____

| Remember | Breakfast | Lunch | Dinner |

Date: _____

Today I am grateful for

_____

_____

To Do List

☐

☐

☐

☐

Chores

_____

_____

_____

My water intake

Notes

_____

_____

_____

_____

_____

Remember	Breakfast	Lunch	Dinner

Date: _____

Today I am grateful for

_____
_____
_____

To Do List

☐
☐
☐
☐

Chores

_____
_____
_____
_____

My water intake

Notes

_____
_____
_____
_____
_____
_____

Remember	Breakfast	Lunch	Dinner

Date: _____

Today I am grateful for

_____

_____

To Do List

☐

☐

☐

☐

Chores

_____

_____

_____

_____

My water intake

Notes

_____

_____

_____

_____

_____

Remember | Breakfast | Lunch | Dinner

Date: _____

Today I am grateful for

_____

_____

To Do List

☐
☐
☐
☐

Chores

_____
_____
_____
_____

My water intake

Notes

_____
_____
_____
_____
_____

| Remember | Breakfast | Lunch | Dinner |

Date: _____

Today I am grateful for

_____

_____

To Do List

☐

☐

☐

☐

Chores

_____

_____

_____

_____

My water intake

Notes

_____

_____

_____

_____

_____

Remember	Breakfast	Lunch	Dinner

Date: _____

Today I am grateful for

_____
_____
_____

To Do List

☐
☐
☐
☐

Chores

_____
_____
_____
_____

My water intake

Notes

_____
_____
_____
_____
_____
_____

Remember	Breakfast	Lunch	Dinner

Date: _____

Today I am grateful for

_____

_____

To Do List

☐
☐
☐
☐

Chores

_____
_____
_____
_____

My water intake

Notes

_____
_____
_____
_____
_____

Remember | Breakfast | Lunch | Dinner

Date: _____

Today I am grateful for

_____

_____

To Do List

☐
☐
☐
☐

Chores

_____
_____
_____
_____

My water intake

Notes

_____

_____

_____

_____

| Remember | Breakfast | Lunch | Dinner |

Date: _____

Today I am grateful for

_____

_____

To Do List

☐

☐

☐

☐

Chores

_____

_____

_____

My water intake

Notes

_____

_____

_____

_____

Remember	Breakfast	Lunch	Dinner

Date: _____

Today I am grateful for

_____

_____

To Do List

- ☐
- ☐
- ☐
- ☐

Chores

_____
_____
_____
_____

My water intake

Notes

_____
_____
_____
_____
_____

Remember	Breakfast	Lunch	Dinner

Date: _____

Today I am grateful for

_____

_____

To Do List

- ☐
- ☐
- ☐
- ☐

Chores

_____

_____

_____

My water intake

Notes

_____

_____

_____

_____

_____

Remember	Breakfast	Lunch	Dinner

Date: _____

Today I am grateful for

_____
_____

To Do List

☐
☐
☐
☐

Chores

_____
_____
_____
_____

My water intake

Notes

_____
_____
_____
_____
_____

Remember	Breakfast	Lunch	Dinner

Date: _____

Today I am grateful for

_____

_____

To Do List

☐
☐
☐
☐

Chores

_____
_____
_____

My water intake

Notes

_____
_____
_____
_____
_____

| Remember | Breakfast | Lunch | Dinner |

Date: _____

Today I am grateful for

_____

_____

To Do List

☐

☐

☐

☐

Chores

_____

_____

_____

_____

My water intake

Notes

_____

_____

_____

_____

_____

Remember	Breakfast	Lunch	Dinner

Date: _____

Today I am grateful for

_____
_____
_____

To Do List

☐
☐
☐
☐

Chores

_____
_____
_____
_____

My water intake

Notes

_____
_____
_____
_____
_____

Remember	Breakfast	Lunch	Dinner

Date: _____

Today I am grateful for

_____

_____

To Do List

☐
☐
☐
☐

Chores

_____
_____
_____
_____
_____

My water intake

Notes

_____
_____
_____
_____
_____

Remember | Breakfast | Lunch | Dinner

Date: _____

Today I am grateful for

_____

_____

To Do List

☐

☐

☐

☐

Chores

_____

_____

_____

My water intake

Notes

_____

_____

_____

_____

_____

| Remember | Breakfast | Lunch | Dinner |

Date: _____

Today I am grateful for

_____

_____

To Do List

☐

☐

☐

☐

Chores

_____

_____

_____

_____

My water intake

Notes

_____

_____

_____

_____

_____

_____

Remember	Breakfast	Lunch	Dinner

Date: _____

Today I am grateful for

To Do List

☐
☐
☐
☐

Chores

_____
_____
_____
_____

My water intake

Notes

| Remember | Breakfast | Lunch | Dinner |

Date: _____

Today I am grateful for

_____

_____

To Do List

☐

☐

☐

☐

Chores

_____

_____

_____

_____

My water intake

Notes

_____

_____

_____

_____

_____

| Remember | Breakfast | Lunch | Dinner |

Date: _____

Today I am grateful for

_____

_____

_____

To Do List

☐
☐
☐
☐

Chores

_____
_____
_____
_____

My water intake

Notes

_____
_____
_____
_____
_____

| Remember | Breakfast | Lunch | Dinner |

Date: _____

Today I am grateful for

_____

_____

_____

To Do List

☐
☐
☐
☐

Chores

_____
_____
_____
_____

My water intake

Notes

_____
_____
_____
_____
_____

Remember | **Breakfast** | **Lunch** | **Dinner**

Date: _____

Today I am grateful for

_____

_____

To Do List

- ☐
- ☐
- ☐
- ☐

Chores

_____
_____
_____
_____

My water intake

Notes

_____
_____
_____
_____
_____

| Remember | Breakfast | Lunch | Dinner |

Date: _____

Today I am grateful for

_____

_____

_____

To Do List

☐
☐
☐
☐

Chores

_____
_____
_____
_____

My water intake

Notes

_____

_____

_____

_____

_____

| Remember | Breakfast | Lunch | Dinner |

Date: _____

Today I am grateful for

_____

_____

_____

To Do List

☐
☐
☐
☐

Chores

_____
_____
_____

My water intake

Notes

_____
_____
_____
_____
_____

| Remember | Breakfast | Lunch | Dinner |

Date: _____

Today I am grateful for

_____
_____
_____

To Do List

- ☐
- ☐
- ☐
- ☐

Chores

_____
_____
_____
_____

My water intake

Notes

_____
_____
_____
_____
_____

| Remember | Breakfast | Lunch | Dinner |

Date: _____

Today I am grateful for

_____

_____

_____

To Do List

Chores

☐ _____

☐ _____

☐ _____

☐ _____

My water intake

Notes

_____

_____

_____

_____

_____

Remember	Breakfast	Lunch	Dinner

Date: _____

Today I am grateful for

_____

_____

_____

To Do List

☐

☐

☐

☐

Chores

_____

_____

_____

_____

My water intake

Notes

_____

_____

_____

_____

_____

Remember	Breakfast	Lunch	Dinner

Date: _____

Today I am grateful for

_____

_____

_____

To Do List

☐

☐

☐

☐

Chores

_____

_____

_____

My water intake

Notes

_____

_____

_____

_____

_____

_____

| Remember | Breakfast | Lunch | Dinner |

Date: _____

Today I am grateful for

_____

_____

_____

To Do List

- ☐
- ☐
- ☐
- ☐

Chores

_____

_____

_____

_____

My water intake

Notes

_____

_____

_____

_____

_____

Remember	Breakfast	Lunch	Dinner

Date: _____

Today I am grateful for

_____

_____

To Do List

☐
☐
☐
☐

Chores

_____
_____
_____
_____

My water intake

Notes

_____
_____
_____
_____
_____

Remember	Breakfast	Lunch	Dinner

Date: _____

Today I am grateful for

_____

_____

_____

To Do List

☐
☐
☐
☐

Chores

_____
_____
_____
_____

My water intake

Notes

_____

_____

_____

_____

_____

Remember	Breakfast	Lunch	Dinner

Date: _____

Today I am grateful for

_____

_____

To Do List

☐
☐
☐
☐

Chores

_____
_____
_____
_____

My water intake

Notes

_____
_____
_____
_____
_____

Remember	Breakfast	Lunch	Dinner

Date: _____

Today I am grateful for

_____

_____

_____

To Do List

☐
☐
☐
☐

Chores

_____

_____

_____

_____

My water intake

Notes

_____

_____

_____

_____

_____

Remember	Breakfast	Lunch	Dinner

Date: _____

Today I am grateful for

_____

_____

To Do List

☐

☐

☐

☐

Chores

_____

_____

_____

My water intake

Notes

_____

_____

_____

_____

_____

Remember	Breakfast	Lunch	Dinner

Date: _____

Today I am grateful for

_____

_____

To Do List

☐

☐

☐

☐

Chores

_____

_____

_____

My water intake

Notes

_____

_____

_____

_____

Remember	Breakfast	Lunch	Dinner

Date: _____

Today I am grateful for

_____

_____

To Do List

☐

☐

☐

☐

Chores

_____

_____

_____

My water intake

Notes

_____

_____

_____

_____

| Remember | Breakfast | Lunch | Dinner |

Date: _____

Today I am grateful for

_____
_____
_____

To Do List

☐
☐
☐
☐

Chores

_____
_____
_____
_____

My water intake

Notes

_____
_____
_____
_____
_____

Remember	Breakfast	Lunch	Dinner

Date: _____

Today I am grateful for

_____

_____

To Do List

☐

☐

☐

☐

Chores

_____

_____

_____

_____

My water intake

Notes

_____

_____

_____

_____

_____

Remember	Breakfast	Lunch	Dinner

Date: _____

Today I am grateful for

_____

_____

_____

To Do List

☐

☐

☐

☐

Chores

_____

_____

_____

My water intake

Notes

_____

_____

_____

_____

_____

Remember	Breakfast	Lunch	Dinner

Date: _____

Today I am grateful for

_____

_____

To Do List

☐

☐

☐

☐

Chores

_____

_____

_____

My water intake

Notes

_____

_____

_____

_____

Remember	Breakfast	Lunch	Dinner

Date: _____

Today I am grateful for

_____

_____

_____

To Do List

☐
☐
☐
☐

Chores

_____
_____
_____
_____

My water intake

Notes

_____

_____

_____

_____

_____

_____

Remember	Breakfast	Lunch	Dinner

Date: _____

Today I am grateful for

_____

_____

To Do List

☐

☐

☐

☐

Chores

_____

_____

_____

_____

My water intake

Notes

_____

_____

_____

_____

_____

Remember	Breakfast	Lunch	Dinner

Date: _____

Today I am grateful for

_____
_____
_____

To Do List

- ☐
- ☐
- ☐
- ☐

Chores

_____
_____
_____
_____

My water intake

Notes

_____
_____
_____
_____
_____

Remember	Breakfast	Lunch	Dinner

Date: _____

Today I am grateful for

_____

_____

To Do List

☐

☐

☐

☐

Chores

_____

_____

_____

_____

My water intake

Notes

_____

_____

_____

_____

_____

Remember	Breakfast	Lunch	Dinner

Date: _____

Today I am grateful for

_____

_____

To Do List

☐
☐
☐
☐

Chores

_____

_____

_____

_____

My water intake

Notes

_____

_____

_____

_____

_____

Remember | Breakfast | Lunch | Dinner

Date: _____

Today I am grateful for

_____

_____

To Do List

- ☐
- ☐
- ☐
- ☐

Chores

_____

My water intake

Notes

_____

_____

_____

_____

Remember | Breakfast | Lunch | Dinner

Date: _____

Today I am grateful for

_____
_____
_____

To Do List

☐
☐
☐
☐

Chores

_____
_____
_____
_____

My water intake

Notes

_____
_____
_____
_____
_____

Remember	Breakfast	Lunch	Dinner

Date: _____

Today I am grateful for

_____

_____

To Do List

☐

☐

☐

☐

Chores

_____

_____

_____

My water intake

Notes

_____

_____

_____

_____

_____

Remember	Breakfast	Lunch	Dinner

Date: _____

Today I am grateful for

_____

_____

_____

To Do List

☐

☐

☐

☐

Chores

_____

_____

_____

_____

My water intake

Notes

_____

_____

_____

_____

_____

| Remember | Breakfast | Lunch | Dinner |

Date: _____

Today I am grateful for

_____

_____

_____

To Do List

☐

☐

☐

☐

Chores

_____

_____

_____

My water intake

Notes

_____

_____

_____

_____

_____

Remember	Breakfast	Lunch	Dinner

Date: _____

Today I am grateful for

_____

_____

To Do List

☐
☐
☐
☐

Chores

_____
_____
_____

My water intake

Notes

_____
_____
_____
_____

| Remember | Breakfast | Lunch | Dinner |

Date: _____

Today I am grateful for

_____

_____

To Do List

- ☐
- ☐
- ☐
- ☐

Chores

_____

_____

_____

_____

My water intake

Notes

_____

_____

_____

_____

Remember	Breakfast	Lunch	Dinner

Date: _____

Today I am grateful for

_____

_____

_____

To Do List

☐

☐

☐

☐

Chores

_____

_____

_____

_____

My water intake

Notes

_____

_____

_____

_____

_____

_____

Remember	Breakfast	Lunch	Dinner

Date: _____

Today I am grateful for

_____
_____
_____

To Do List

- [ ]
- [ ]
- [ ]
- [ ]

Chores

_____
_____
_____

My water intake

Notes

_____
_____
_____
_____
_____

Remember	Breakfast	Lunch	Dinner

Date: _____

Today I am grateful for

_____

_____

_____

To Do List

☐
☐
☐
☐

Chores

_____
_____
_____
_____

My water intake

Notes

_____
_____
_____
_____
_____

| Remember | Breakfast | Lunch | Dinner |

Date: _____

Today I am grateful for

_____

_____

To Do List

☐

☐

☐

☐

Chores

_____
_____
_____
_____

My water intake

Notes

_____

_____

_____

_____

_____

Remember	Breakfast	Lunch	Dinner

Date: _____

Today I am grateful for

_____

_____

_____

To Do List

☐
☐
☐
☐

Chores

_____
_____
_____
_____

My water intake

Notes

_____
_____
_____
_____
_____

Remember | Breakfast | Lunch | Dinner

Date: _____

Today I am grateful for

_____
_____

To Do List

☐
☐
☐
☐

Chores

_____
_____
_____

My water intake

Notes

_____
_____
_____
_____

Remember	Breakfast	Lunch	Dinner

Date: _____

Today I am grateful for

_____
_____

To Do List

☐
☐
☐
☐

Chores

_____
_____
_____
_____

My water intake

Notes

_____
_____
_____
_____
_____
_____

Remember	Breakfast	Lunch	Dinner

Date: _____

Today I am grateful for

_____

_____

To Do List

☐

☐

☐

☐

Chores

_____

_____

_____

_____

My water intake

Notes

_____

_____

_____

_____

Remember	Breakfast	Lunch	Dinner

Date: _____

Today I am grateful for

_____

_____

_____

To Do List

☐

☐

☐

☐

Chores

_____

_____

_____

_____

My water intake

Notes

_____

_____

_____

_____

_____

| Remember | Breakfast | Lunch | Dinner |

Date: _____

Today I am grateful for

_____

_____

To Do List

☐

☐

☐

☐

Chores

_____

_____

_____

_____

My water intake

Notes

_____

_____

_____

_____

_____

Remember	Breakfast	Lunch	Dinner

Date: _____

Today I am grateful for

_____
_____
_____

To Do List

☐
☐
☐
☐

Chores

_____
_____
_____
_____

My water intake

Notes

_____
_____
_____
_____
_____

Remember	Breakfast	Lunch	Dinner

Date: _____

Today I am grateful for

_____

_____

To Do List

☐

☐

☐

☐

Chores

_____

_____

_____

_____

My water intake

Notes

_____

_____

_____

_____

_____

| Remember | Breakfast | Lunch | Dinner |

Date: _____

Today I am grateful for

_____

_____

_____

To Do List

☐
☐
☐
☐

Chores

_____
_____
_____
_____

My water intake

Notes

_____

_____

_____

_____

_____

Remember	Breakfast	Lunch	Dinner

Date: _____

Today I am grateful for

_____

_____

To Do List

☐

☐

☐

☐

Chores

_____

_____

_____

My water intake

Notes

_____

_____

_____

_____

_____

Remember	Breakfast	Lunch	Dinner

Date: _____

Today I am grateful for

_____

_____

_____

To Do List

- ☐
- ☐
- ☐
- ☐

Chores

_____

_____

_____

_____

My water intake

Notes

_____

_____

_____

_____

Remember	Breakfast	Lunch	Dinner

Date: _____

Today I am grateful for

_____

_____

To Do List

☐

☐

☐

☐

Chores

_____

_____

_____

_____

My water intake

Notes

_____

_____

_____

_____

_____

Remember	Breakfast	Lunch	Dinner

Date: _____

Today I am grateful for

_____

_____

_____

To Do List

- ☐
- ☐
- ☐
- ☐

Chores

_____

_____

_____

_____

My water intake

Notes

_____

_____

_____

_____

_____

Remember	Breakfast	Lunch	Dinner

Date: _____

Today I am grateful for

_____

_____

_____

To Do List

- ☐
- ☐
- ☐
- ☐

Chores

_____

_____

_____

My water intake

Notes

_____

_____

_____

_____

_____

Remember	Breakfast	Lunch	Dinner

Date: _____

Today I am grateful for

_____

_____

To Do List

☐
☐
☐
☐

Chores

_____

_____

_____

_____

My water intake

Notes

_____

_____

_____

_____

_____

| Remember | Breakfast | Lunch | Dinner |

Date: _____

Today I am grateful for

_____

_____

To Do List

☐
☐
☐
☐

Chores

_____
_____
_____

My water intake

Notes

_____
_____
_____
_____
_____

| Remember | Breakfast | Lunch | Dinner |

Date: _____

Today I am grateful for

_____

_____

To Do List

☐
☐
☐
☐

Chores

_____

_____

_____

_____

My water intake

Notes

_____

_____

_____

_____

| Remember | Breakfast | Lunch | Dinner |

Date: _____

Today I am grateful for

_____

_____

_____

To Do List

☐

☐

☐

☐

Chores

_____

_____

_____

_____

My water intake

Notes

_____

_____

_____

_____

_____

Remember	Breakfast	Lunch	Dinner

Date: _____

Today I am grateful for

_____
_____
_____

To Do List

☐
☐
☐
☐

Chores

_____
_____
_____
_____

My water intake

Notes

_____
_____
_____
_____
_____
_____

| Remember | Breakfast | Lunch | Dinner |

Date: _____

Today I am grateful for

_____

_____

_____

To Do List

☐

☐

☐

☐

Chores

_____

_____

_____

My water intake

Notes

_____

_____

_____

_____

Remember	Breakfast	Lunch	Dinner

Date: _____

Today I am grateful for

_____

_____

_____

To Do List

☐
☐
☐
☐

Chores

_____
_____
_____
_____

My water intake

Notes

_____
_____
_____
_____
_____

| Remember | Breakfast | Lunch | Dinner |

Date: _____

Today I am grateful for

_____

_____

To Do List

☐
☐
☐
☐

Chores

_____
_____
_____
_____

My water intake

Notes

_____
_____
_____
_____
_____

Remember	Breakfast	Lunch	Dinner

Date: _____

Today I am grateful for

_____

_____

_____

To Do List

☐

☐

☐

☐

Chores

_____

_____

_____

_____

My water intake

Notes

_____

_____

_____

_____

_____

Remember	Breakfast	Lunch	Dinner

Date: _____

Today I am grateful for

_____

_____

_____

To Do List

☐
☐
☐
☐

Chores

_____

_____

_____

_____

My water intake

Notes

_____

_____

_____

_____

_____

| Remember | Breakfast | Lunch | Dinner |

Date: _____

Today I am grateful for

_____

_____

To Do List

☐
☐
☐
☐

Chores

_____
_____
_____
_____

My water intake

Notes

_____
_____
_____
_____
_____

| Remember | Breakfast | Lunch | Dinner |

Date: _____

Today I am grateful for

_____

_____

To Do List

- ☐
- ☐
- ☐
- ☐

Chores

_____

_____

_____

My water intake

Notes

_____

_____

_____

_____

_____

| Remember | Breakfast | Lunch | Dinner |

Date: _____

Today I am grateful for

_____

_____

To Do List

☐
☐
☐
☐

Chores

_____
_____
_____
_____

My water intake

Notes

_____
_____
_____
_____
_____

Remember	Breakfast	Lunch	Dinner

Date: _____

Today I am grateful for

_____

_____

_____

To Do List

☐

☐

☐

☐

Chores

_____

_____

_____

_____

My water intake

Notes

_____

_____

_____

_____

_____

| Remember | Breakfast | Lunch | Dinner |

Date: _____

Today I am grateful for

_____
_____
_____

To Do List

☐
☐
☐
☐

Chores

_____
_____
_____
_____

My water intake

Notes

_____
_____
_____
_____
_____
_____

Remember

Breakfast

Lunch

Dinner

Date: _____

Today I am grateful for

_____

_____

_____

To Do List

☐

☐

☐

☐

Chores

_____

_____

_____

My water intake

Notes

_____

_____

_____

_____

_____

Remember	Breakfast	Lunch	Dinner

Date: _____

Today I am grateful for

_____

_____

To Do List

☐
☐
☐
☐

Chores

_____
_____
_____
_____

My water intake

Notes

_____

_____

_____

_____

_____

Remember	Breakfast	Lunch	Dinner

Date: _____

Today I am grateful for

_____

_____

To Do List

☐
☐
☐
☐

Chores

_____
_____
_____
_____

My water intake

Notes

_____
_____
_____
_____
_____

Remember | Breakfast | Lunch | Dinner

Date: _____

Today I am grateful for

_____

_____

To Do List

☐
☐
☐
☐

Chores

_____
_____
_____
_____

My water intake

Notes

_____
_____
_____
_____
_____

| Remember | Breakfast | Lunch | Dinner |

Date: _____

Today I am grateful for

_____

_____

_____

To Do List

☐

☐

☐

☐

Chores

_____

_____

_____

_____

My water intake

Notes

_____

_____

_____

_____

_____

_____

| Remember | Breakfast | Lunch | Dinner |

Date: _____

Today I am grateful for

_____

_____

_____

To Do List

☐

☐

☐

☐

Chores

_____

_____

_____

_____

My water intake

Notes

_____

_____

_____

_____

_____

Remember	Breakfast	Lunch	Dinner

Date: _____

Today I am grateful for

_____

_____

_____

To Do List

☐

☐

☐

☐

Chores

_____

_____

_____

_____

My water intake

Notes

_____

_____

_____

_____

_____

Remember	Breakfast	Lunch	Dinner

Date: _____

Today I am grateful for

_____
_____
_____

To Do List

☐
☐
☐
☐

Chores

_____
_____
_____
_____

My water intake

Notes

_____
_____
_____
_____
_____

Remember	Breakfast	Lunch	Dinner

Date: _____

Today I am grateful for

_____

_____

To Do List

☐

☐

☐

☐

Chores

_____

_____

_____

My water intake

Notes

_____

_____

_____

_____

Remember	Breakfast	Lunch	Dinner

Date: _____

Today I am grateful for

_____

_____

To Do List

☐
☐
☐
☐

Chores

_____

_____

_____

My water intake

Notes

_____

_____

_____

_____

_____

| Remember | Breakfast | Lunch | Dinner |

Made in the USA
Las Vegas, NV
01 December 2020